Opera Favorites: Powers of Darkness

Powers of Darkness

The idea of the supernatural has long exerted a powerful influence on the artistic imagination, and the dark forces it unleashes have inspired awe, fear and heated debate. In Offenbach's musical masterpiece, *The Tales of Hoffmann*, the dark forces serve to reveal the secret life of the artist—subtle and sinister at the same time. The overpowering atmosphere of Weber's *Der Freischütz*—"The Freeshooter" who gambles with the forces of darkness— thrills and chills as it evokes primeval terror. By contrast, Gounod's *Faust* is almost worldly, portraying the grasp of evil over simple, innocent lives, all the while embracing deep emotional truths with its seductive melodies.

What the Symbols Mean

The Composers
Their lives...
their loves...
their legacies...

The Music
Explanation...
analysis...
interpretation...

The Story
The plot
of the opera,
act by act

The Inspiration
How works
of genius came
to be written

The Background
People, places,
and events linked
to the music

© MCMXCIX IMP AB   In Classical Mood™ IMP AB, produced under license by IMP Inc.   Printed in China.   US P 2201 12 058

Contents

– 3 –
The Tales of Hoffmann by Jacques Offenbach
INTRODUCTION

– 4 –
THE STORY
Unlucky in Love

– 6 –
LISTENER'S GUIDE
Through a Glass, Darkly

– 8 –
IN CONTEXT
The Tale of Hoffmann

– 11 –
Faust by Charles Gounod
INTRODUCTION

– 12 –
THE STORY
Prince of Darkness

– 14 –
LISTENER'S GUIDE
The Price of Pleasure

– 16 –
IN CONTEXT
French Style

– 19 –
Der Freischütz by Carl Maria von Weber
INTRODUCTION

– 20 –
THE STORY
The Malevolent Seven

– 22 –
LISTENER'S GUIDE
A Date with the Devil

– 24 –
IN CONTEXT
Hitting the Target

The Tales of Hoffmann

Jacques Offenbach 1819–1880

A sinister shadow lies over this story of a poet's doomed search for love. For, as Offenbach worked on his one serious opera, he knew that he was dying. His artistic imagination was concerned with the supernatural, love and art, good and evil.

Last Chance

By 1877, Offenbach was plagued by ill health and bad luck. Already the "thinnest man in Paris" (*below*), he was crippled by gout and badly in debt. Haunted by fear that the fame garnered through his light, frivolous operettas might perish with him, he decided to write a serious opera, a task he had both relished and dreaded all his life. In October, he began *Les Contes d'Hoffmann* ("The Tales of Hoffmann"). The stories of the German writer, E.T.A. Hoffmann, were hugely popular in France and, in 1851, Michel Carré and Jules Barbier had written a play based on them. Carré was now dead, but Barbier reworked the play into a libretto. Offenbach spent more time composing this opera than any of his other more breezy offerings. He even managed to compose two more operas while lavishing care and attention on the *Tales*. Unfortunately, the Théâtre-Lyrique, which was to produce the work, went bankrupt and the rights were sold to the Opéra-Comique. Offenbach now had to re-write the music to show off its star singers. "My only wish is to attend the opening night," he wrote. But the premiere was on February 10, 1881—four months after his death, on October 5, 1880.

THE STORY OF THE TALES OF HOFFMANN

Unlucky in Love

Weaving in and out of the supernatural, Hoffmann, a poet, recounts his three great love affairs. In each, he unsuccessfully pursues a beautiful woman—but is she merely another aspect of a former lover, Stella? In each, a wicked, magical figure thwarts him—but does that represent the poet's rival, Lindorf, or Hoffmann's alter ego?

PRINCIPAL CHARACTERS

Hoffmann: a poet;
Nicklaus: Hoffman's friend;
Stella: a singer and Hoffmann's former love; **Olympia, Giulietta, Antonia:** roles assumed by Stella in Hoffmann's stories;
Lindorf: Hoffmann's rival;
Coppélius, Dapertutto, Dr. Miracle: roles of Lindorf in Hoffmann's stories;
The Muse of Poetry

LIVING DOLL

ACT I & II

Hoffmann sits desperate in a tavern in Nuremberg. Unknown to him, Lindorf has intercepted a note from Stella. Urged to sing by his drinking companions, Hoffmann begins but soon drifts off into a reverie about a woman he once loved, and he recounts his adventures. Act II depicts Hoffmann's first love affair: Despite being cautioned by Nicklaus, Hoffmann has fallen in love with Olympia, not realizing that she is a mechanical doll. She sings beautifully and Hoffmann is entranced. In fact, viewing her through magical spectacles that Coppélius sold to him, he is even more bewitched (*left*). But his dreams are literally shattered when the spectacles break and Coppélius smashes the doll.

THE STORY OF THE TALES OF HOFFMANN

VENETIAN GLASS

ACT III

Hoffmann's next adventure takes place in Venice, where he falls in love with the glamorous courtesan, Giulietta. But she is under the power of a magician, Dapertutto, who uses her to capture men's souls. He entices Giulietta with a diamond which she can use to obtain Hoffmann's soul by stealing his reflection. Giulietta seduces Hoffmann who discovers that she has captured his soul—he can no longer see himself in the mirror (*right*). Schlemil, also in love with Giulietta, quarrels with Hoffmann who kills him. Giulietta disappears in a gondola with another man.

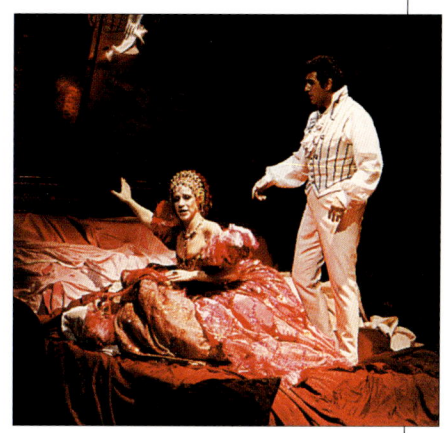

SUNG TO DEATH

ACT IV

Hoffmann's third love is Antonia, a singer who must never sing again. As her father Crespel reminds her, she must not tax her health. But, once again, a malign power intervenes. The sinister Dr. Miracle pretends to treat Antonia, and evokes the ghost of her mother, who implores her to sing. Antonia cannot resist, sings and dies (*left*). Back in Luther's tavern, Nicklaus dares to suggest that Hoffmann's three loves were all manifestations of Stella. Angry and drunk, Hoffmann falls into a stupor. But he has not lost everything: the Muse of Poetry comes to claim him, for pain has made him a true poet. A gloating Lindorf claims Stella. As she leaves with him, she cannot take her eyes off Hoffman.

Listener's Guide to The Tales of Hoffmann

Through a Glass, Darkly

THE LEGEND OF KLEINZACH: VA POUR KLEINZACH!

TRACK 1 ACT I — Prevailed upon by the company at the tavern to sing, Hoffmann consents, "Right, then, Kleinzach it is," (*left*). The catchy, merry tune is about a dwarf whose knees went "Clic-clac! Clic-clac!" and his head, "Crick-crack! Crick-crack!" The drinkers echo Hoffmann enthusiastically. "As for the face…" suddenly, in strong contrast to the raucous drinking song, Hoffmann slips off into a wistful daydream about a woman he loved. A puzzled companion, Nathanaël, wants to know what is going on. Hoffmann quickly recovers and returns to Kleinzach.

THE DOLL SONG: LES OISEAUX DANS LA CHARMILLE

TRACK 2 ACT II — In this showpiece aria, the beautiful Olympia (*right*) performs before her guests. "The birds in the bower, the sun in the heavens," everything speaks to a maiden of love. The pretty, dainty piece goes with her stilted demeanour, but the enthralled Hoffmann does not realize that she is a doll. Offenbach used this particular kind of soprano voice—the coloratura—with its superhuman, dazzling quality to hint at the disturbing truth about Olympia. She is mesmerizing but has no soul: the music is artful but her words are empty. Eerily, her voice weakens now and then, until a tap to her shoulder winds up her spring mechanism, and off she goes trilling again.

Barcarolle: Belle nuit, ô nuit d'amour

In a palace in Venice overlooking the Grand Canal, a gorgeously attired company listens to a barcarolle, a Venetian boat-song. "Lovely night, O night of love" has been described by the critic, Stephen Williams, as "the most insidious expression of sheer languid voluptuousness in all opera." These ravishing sounds come from two "voices" off-stage, one of whom is revealed at the end as the hostess, Giulietta. Millions worldwide who have never heard of Offenbach hum this romantic melody.

Scintille, diamant!

At Giulietta's ball in Venice, everyone has departed to the gaming tables leaving behind the sorcerer, Dapertutto (*below*). Drawing out a large diamond, he sings this powerful aria.

"Sparkle, diamond!" he commands the magic stone. Like a mirror that traps a lark, this intriguing gem can tempt a woman to lose her soul. Once he has captured Giulietta's with it, he will get her to destroy Hoffmann.

Écoute!

Antonia is forbidden to sing lest the exertion should kill her. But "Listen!" sings the evil Dr. Miracle, conjuring up the voice of her dead mother, herself a brilliant singer. Her mother's image glows with life as she calls out to her daughter. Dr. Miracle insists that her mother left Antonia her talent, and he

begins to play on a violin. Antonia cannot resist and begins to sing. Panting, Antonia says she should not, but the ethereal mother urges her on. This haunting trio goes on until Antonia collapses (*above*). Dr. Miracle disappears into the earth shouting with laughter, as the mother's voice and vision fade away.

In Context: The Tales of Hoffmann

The Tale of Hoffmann

The extraordinary Ernst Theodor Willhelm Hoffmann was born on January 24, 1776, in Königsberg, Germany. (Later in life, he dropped Willhelm and adopted Amadeus in homage to his revered Mozart.) E.T.A. Hoffmann was a brilliant writer who created outrageous fantasies blended with psychology and philosophy. He came from a broken home and was brought up by a tyrannical uncle who seems to recur in his nephew's stories as an evil man who ruins happiness. What tenderness and indulgence the boy knew came from his aunt, Sophia, a talented singer. For Hoffmann, love and singing were to be forever twined. In addition to being a great writer, he was also a talented artist. Music was his first and greatest love: his opera *Undine* (1816) was greatly admired by Weber. It is only fitting that the man and his talents are celebrated in opera.

Hoffmann qualified as a lawyer and eventually became a judge of the Supreme Court in Berlin but, alongside this, he maintained his artistic—and amorous—pursuits. He had many love affairs, which he translated into his stories, but he was also happily married, and his wife can often be detected in his writings as the good woman from whom he strays. Perhaps it is no surprise that he burnt himself out by the age of 46, although more precise accounts blame his death on syphilis and drink. Hoffmann's writings influenced many writers and musicians, among them, Delibes, whose ballet, *Coppélia*, featured a mechanical doll (*right*).

IN CONTEXT: THE TALES OF HOFFMANN

EVER-CHANGING

Offenbach revised and altered his works up to—and often after—their first performance. So it was no surprise that *The Tales of Hoffmann* was still incomplete when he died. Ernest Guiraud was asked to complete the orchestration. He brought in sung recitatives in place of dialogue, as Offenbach had intended. But the original third (Giulietta) act (*right*) created problems. Offenbach had not completed her solo, and it was decided to cut out the whole act. The Muse was removed from the first act, and Hoffmann's sensual love-song to Giulietta was turned into a surprisingly erotic prayer to the Muse at the end. None of this affected the success of the opera, and it continued to change through the years. In 1905, Hans Gregor in Berlin reinstated the Giulietta act, although he put it before the Antonia act. After World War II, Fritz Oeser made a new edition, reworking Offenbach's original material.

CYCLE OF SUCCESS

Greeted with universal acclaim at its first production in early 1881, *The Tales of Hoffmann* played 101 times that year at the Opéra-Comique in Paris. In December, it opened in Vienna, but a huge fire on the second night killed hundreds of people. Fear of a jinx on the opera delayed further productions. But it opened in New York in 1882, in Berlin two years later and, perhaps most famously, under the baton of Sir Thomas Beecham in London in 1910. In 1951, Beecham directed the soundtrack when the opera was filmed with dancers Moira Shearer, Robert Helpmann, Leonide Massine and Frederick Ashton miming the roles to other voices.

KEY NOTES

Offenbach wanted one soprano to sing the role of Stella and all three heroines. But few singers could cope with such lyrical, dramatic and pyrotechnical demands. In modern times, Anna Moffo, Beverly Sills and Joan Sutherland are among those who have managed to do so.

Faust

Charles Gounod 1818–1893

In *Faust*, Gounod took the supernatural and turned it into songs. The timeless and fascinating themes— the seductive power of evil and the struggle for salvation, along with a love story and a pact with the Devil—are all filled with human emotion.

Date with the Devil

Gounod had been enthralled by Gœthe's poetic drama, *Faust*, since the age of 20, but it was more than 15 years before he realized his dream of turning it into an opera. The project began to take off when he met the successful librettist, Jules Barbier (*right*), who had exactly the same ambition. Barbier wrote the text, and Carvalho, director of the Théâtre-Lyrique in Paris, agreed to stage the opera. It was soon postponed because a rival adaptation with music was about to be staged. Gounod was miserable, but consoled himself with writing another opera, *Le Médecin malgré lui* ("The Reluctant Doctor"), his first success.

Carvalho decided to launch *Faust* at the end of 1858, but there were numerous delays. The Minister of Fine Arts wanted the church scene cut in case it offended the Vatican. But the Papal Ambassador, a friend of Gounod, sanctioned it. Then the vain and imperious Madame Carvalho, who was to play Marguerite, spent large amounts of time "improving" her part. Hector Guardi, who was to be Faust, lost his voice at the last minute and had to be replaced. Gounod made cuts to the score, but somehow believed it would "all come right... on the first night." On March 19, 1859, he was proven right.

THE STORY OF FAUST

Prince of Darkness

The legend of the man who sells his soul to the Devil for knowledge or power is both ancient and awesome. Gounod's Faust, having spent his life in arid learning, now regrets missing the sensual pleasures of youth and has more carnal considerations on his mind.

A FATAL SIGNATURE

ACT I

At dawn one day, in a 16th-century German village, old Faust reflects on his past, and is ready to take his own life. In his despair, he curses all belief and calls on the Devil. Mephistopheles promptly appears and offers his services. He agrees to give Faust back his youth, in exchange for Faust's soul after his death. Faust signs a contract to this effect, spurred on by a vision of the lovely Marguerite (*right*). He drinks the Devil's elixir of youth, which turns him into a handsome young man ready for adventure.

PRINCIPAL CHARACTERS

Faust: an aged scholar;
Mephistopheles: the Devil;
Marguerite: a village girl;
Valentin: her brother, a soldier;
Siebel: his friend, in love with Marguerite

12

THE STORY OF FAUST

IRRESISTIBLE TEMPTATION

ACT II & III

People are making merry at the Easter fair. Valentin, who is about to go to war, is worried about leaving Marguerite on her own, but his friend, Siebel, who loves her, reassures him. Mephistopheles joins them and raises a toast to Marguerite. Outraged, Valentin draws his sword, but his blade breaks into pieces. Faust enters and begs the Devil to lead him to the girl of his vision. As couples begin to dance, she appears, but innocently refuses Faust's advances (*right*). In Act III, Mephistopheles gives Faust a casket of jewels to tempt Marguerite. She is thrilled and, with Mephistopheles's help, Faust wins her trust and she responds to his wooing. She insists on retiring for the night but, as he waits, he hears her pour out her love for him. He calls to her, and they fall into each other's arms.

DISGRACE AND DAMNATION

ACT IV & V

Marguerite is praying in church, when Mephistopheles appears to tell her she is doomed. Valentin, returning from war, is appalled at his sister's seduction, and fights a duel with Faust in which Valentin is mortally wounded. Valentin curses Marguerite with his dying breath. Act V opens with the ghostly Walpurgis Night celebrations, at which a vision of Marguerite appears. Faust insists on seeing her, and they discover her in prison for the murder of her baby (*left*). She has gone mad with grief, but refuses to accompany Faust and Mephistopheles. The angels proclaim her salvation, while the Devil claims Faust for himself.

Listener's Guide to Faust

The Price of Pleasure

À MOI LES PLAISIRS

Track 6, Act 1 — Mephistopheles has responded to Faust's summons, and now the old scholar tells him what he wants more than gold, glory or power—youth. In this fantasy of a song, he exults at the thought that "pleasure will be mine," nothing less than a "mad orgy of the heart and senses." The Devil agrees to grant it all, casually informing Faust that, in return, "down there, you will be mine." Shaken, Faust hesitates to sign the fateful parchment signifying their bargain. But his fear vanishes when a vision of the lovely Marguerite is conjured up by Mephistopheles. Faust signs, drinks the Devil's potion and is instantly turned into an elegant, young lord. The diabolical two trip away merrily chanting of the delights to come.

LE VEAU D'OR EST TOUJOURS DEBOUT!

Track 7, Act 1 — In this aria, Mephistopheles (*above*) fascinates the holiday crowd. "The golden calf is still standing," he sings, meaning the god of wealth. It leads everyone into a frenzied dance, with Satan at its head—and likewise, the people fall in with his tune and echo his words.

AINSI QUE LA BRISE LÉGÈRE

Track 8, Act 1 — The townsfolk dance to a waltz that wafts them away "like the light breeze." Mephistopheles tempts Faust with one of the girls, but he can dream only of Marguerite. Siebel says that Marguerite will pass by, and as the waltz melody returns, she appears, a vision of grace and beauty.

Listener's Guide to Faust

Jewel Song: Un bouquet!... O Dieu! Que de bijoux!

The most famous aria in this opera is Marguerite's. She finds a bouquet from Siebel, and next to it a casket of jewels left by Faust. Gingerly, she opens it and naively exclaims on looking inside, "Good Heavens! What a lot of jewels!" There is a mirror laid at the bottom of the casket. She tries on a pair of earrings, and laughs at her lovely reflection (*left*). Her thoughts turn to the handsome stranger who accosted her in the square the evening before. "If only he could see me like this, as beautiful as any young lady!" She puts on all the jewelery...and the Devil's work is almost complete.

Seigneur, daignez permettre... Souviens-toi du passé

After her seduction and betrayal by Faust, Marguerite prays in the church, "Lord, allow your humble servant to kneel before you." But Mephistopheles summons the demons to distract and terrify her. "Remember the past," he says, when she was able to pray in all innocence (*right*). But now, hell awaits her.

Alerte, alerte, ou vous êtes perdus... Anges purs!... Sauvée! Christ est ressuscité!

"Take care, or you are lost," says Mephistopheles and, with Faust tries to persuade Marguerite to flee with them. But she recognizes the Devil and calls upon the "pure angels" to carry her up to heaven. She recoils from Faust, whose hands have blood on them. As she falls senseless, the angels sing, "Saved! Christ has risen!" in an uplifting chorus.

In Context: Faust

French Style

The story of the scholar who sells his soul to the Devil is based on a real man, Georg Faust, who lived in Germany from about 1488 to 1541. He was a doctor, magician, astrologer and alchemist, and was considered learned but of evil reputation. Nevertheless, he quickly became a legendary figure, thanks to the *Faustbuch* compiled by Johann Speis in 1587, a collection of ancient occult tales attributed to Faust. This was widely translated and inspired imaginative versions of the Faust legend, such as Christopher Marlowe's play, *Dr Faustus*, published in 1604 (frontispiece, *right*), which imbued the story with a tragic dignity. Gœthe's dramatic poem, *Faust* (1832), written over 60 years, is complex and rich in symbolism, dealing with the conflict between human thought and action. It is considered the greatest work in German literature.

A Rare Woman

While he was living in London during the Franco-Prussian war, Gounod fell for the beautiful singer, Georgina Weldon (cartoon, *left*). She was equally impressed by him at their first meeting, bursting into tears when he sang. Weldon was forceful rather than sensual, and though she took Gounod into her house, while his wife returned to Paris, their relationship was platonic. She looked after his frail health, wrestled him to the ground when he threatened to burn his manuscripts, and sang his work to great acclaim. However, Gounod eventually rejoined his wife, and Weldon spent much of her life afterward pursuing him with a huge bill for her loving care.

In Context: Faust

Fun with Faust

Faust with a French twist seems to have been Gounod's intention in creating an opera from the only romantic episode in Gœthe's deeply serious poem. In so doing he gave the French tradition of grand opera a new direction. True feeling replaced pomposity, and intimacy took over from spectacle. Mephistopheles is an intelligent comedian, young and rather attractive, who indulges in ironic flirtation. Ostensibly a morality tale, Gounod's *Faust* is a simple love story that uses the devil for picturesque effect. Gounod (*right*, with "muses") was himself famous for his many liaisons and his susceptibility to pretty women and nubile girls.

Delayed Reaction

Faust made a surprisingly quiet entry into the world, playing for a respectable 59 performances. Wagner scornfully called it "a theatrical parody of our Faust." Soon the opera traveled to New York and London. However, when the director of the Théâtre-Lyrique went bankrupt in 1868, the Paris Opera took up the work. At their insistence, Gounod wrote a new ballet sequence, and dialogue was replaced by recitative. In this new version, *Faust* was a huge success. Illustrious sopranos have sung the role of Marguerite, including Kiri Te Kanawa (*left*).

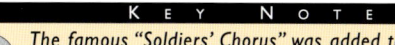

Key Notes
The famous "Soldiers' Chorus" was added to Faust as an afterthought. At a party, Gounod played a piece from his unfinished opera, Ivan the Terrible. His guests insisted he include it in Faust. Wisely, he took the advice.

Der Freischütz

Carl Maria von Weber 1786–1826

The "Freeshooter" of the title was, in European legend, a marksman who made a pact with the Devil to obtain magic bullets. The twist to the bargain was that the Devil could aim the last, seventh, bullet at a target of his own choice.

A Sure Aim

As early as the 14th century, legends about the Freischütz (freeshooter) were common in Germany. Weber (*below*, with characters from *Der Freischütz*) read a version in the 1811 *Gespensterbuch* ("Book of Ghosts") by Johann August Apel and Friedrich Laun, and immediately thought of turning the story into an opera. He revived the idea in 1817, when he met the writer, Johann Friedrich Kind, who speedily produced a libretto. Kind set the story in the mid-17th century, when superstition was prevalent. Weber took three years to write the score, for his duties as Kapellmeister (Music Director) in Dresden were exacting. He began with the part of Ännchen, who resembled his bride-to-be, Caroline Brandt. *Freischütz* was to be the first opera staged in the new Berlin Theater. Italian opera had a fanatical following there, and it seemed that Weber's opera might be overshadowed. Despite the audacious novelty of the music and feeble stage effects, the opera was received, as Weber wrote, "with incredible enthusiasm."

THE STORY OF DER FREISCHÜTZ

The Malevolent Seven

A young man will go to extraordinary lengths to win the woman he loves—even deal with the Devil. Max must win a shooting-trial to convince Kuno that he is a suitable husband for his daughter, Agathe. But Max seems jinxed—he cannot shoot straight. Kaspar comes to his aid and offers to provide magic bullets. But there is a price to be paid: a meeting in the haunted Wolf's Glen at midnight, with the demonic Samiel.

PRINCIPAL CHARACTERS

Max: a huntsman; **Kuno:** the head ranger; **Agathe:** his daughter; **Ännchen:** her friend; **Kaspar:** an evil huntsman; **Samiel:** The demon Black Hunter; **Ottokar:** Prince of Bohemia; **The Hermit**

MISSED, AGAIN

ACT I

It is not Max's day. He has missed with every single shot in a shooting competition and is being teased by the village folk (*left*). And if he fares as badly the next day in the trial before the Prince, he will lose his beloved Agathe to the victor. Kaspar, who is in league with the powers of evil gives him his own gun to shoot a bird so far away it can hardly be seen. A golden eagle falls at their feet. Kaspar reveals that the gun was loaded with a magic bullet. If Max wants more of these, he must meet Kaspar at the Wolf's Glen at midnight—when the doors of hell open.

THE STORY OF DER FREISCHÜTZ

THE GHOSTLY GLEN

ACT II

In Agathe's cottage, a portrait has inexplicably fallen off the wall and hurt her. She feels uneasy, she tells Ännchen, because the Hermit, who gave her roses, warned her of unknown danger. When Max arrives and recounts the story of his golden eagle, they realize that Agathe was hurt at the very moment that he shot the bird. Now Agathe is even more frightened but, despite her pleas, Max leaves for the the Wolf's Glen. There, Kaspar is arranging a deal with the demon, Samiel. He offers Max as prey in place of himself, and asks Samiel for seven magic bullets: the seventh will be the demon's—to kill Agathe. When Max arrives, terrified by the eerie surroundings, he sees ghostly visions of his mother and Agathe. Against a raging tempest and a phantom hunt, Kaspar casts the magic bullets. With the seventh, Samiel appears (*left*).

THE TRIUMPH OF GOOD

ACT III

Kaspar has tricked Max, leaving him the last bullet—the one pledged to Samiel. Meanwhile, Agathe is still uneasy. She has dreamt that she was a white dove that Max shot. At the contest, Prince Ottokar commands Max to shoot a white dove perched on a tree. Agathe arrives just as his shot rings out. Both she and Kaspar fall. But Agathe has only fainted (*right*). The bullet found Kaspar, who hid himself behind the tree. As he lies wounded, Samiel arrives to claim his soul. The Prince is angry at Max for using magic bullets, but asks the Hermit to pass judgement. He abolishes shooting-trials and asks the Prince to allow Max to marry Agathe after a year's probation. The Prince agrees.

A Date with the Devil

Durch die Wälder, durch die Auen

Young Max (*left*) is in despair. He cannot live without Agathe, his love, but he has lost his cunning as a marksman and without it he cannot win her hand. He begins this aria with a beautiful melody, "through the forests, through the meadows," as he remembers a time when he was light-hearted, a successful hunter who brought a rich bag home to his love at the end of the day. The music then takes on a more sinister turn as the diabolical Samiel hovers in the background, unseen by the troubled Max, who pours out his fear of being abandoned by Providence. In his torment, he asks, "Is there no God?" At the sound of this name, the evil Samiel vanishes with a convulsion.

Wie nahte mir der Schlummer... Leise, leise, fromme Weise

"How did sleep come to me before I saw him?" wonders Agathe (*right*) as she waits for Max. She goes out on to her balcony and, in rapture at the beauty of the night, intones a simple but exquisite prayer. "Softly, softly, my pure song!" she sings, hoping her words waft to heaven, begging God for protection even as she senses danger looming in her life. Finally she glimpses Max, his hat adorned with flowers. This means his luck has returned and, in an ecstatic passage, Agathe sings of her renewed hope and courage. She thanks heaven, for tomorrow, the day of his contest, his shot will be sure. Her pulse racing, she prepares to greet her beloved.

THE WOLF'S GLEN

The terrible Wolf's Glen is the realm of Samiel. Here, Kaspar has laid out a circle of black boulders, a skull and some eagle feathers, preparing to cast the magic bullets. As he works, the voices of invisible spirits rise in a menacing chant, "Before the evening falls again... will the gentle bride be slain! Before the next descent of night, will the sacrifice be done!" After Max has arrived, scared out of his wits by the grotesque visions he has seen, Kaspar begins to cast the magic bullets. He counts them one by one, to the echo of an unearthly voice. The music mingles with the sounds of a rising storm and a chorus of ghostly huntsmen. As the seventh bullet ("Sieben!"), the devil's own, is cast, the scene explodes with thunder and lightning, and Kaspar is thrown to the ground (*above*). "Samiel!" screams Max and the Black Huntsman emerges, reaching out for his hand. Max makes the sign of the cross and collapses.

WAS GLEICHT WOHL AUF ERDEN

The shooting contest, the climax of the opera, is about to begin (*right*). But the huntsmen are in the mood for celebration. They launch into a spirited chorus, "What pleasure on earth can compare with the hunter's?" As they extol the thrill of the chase, they raise their goblets, and the world of Samiel seems very far away.

IN CONTEXT: DER FREISCHÜTZ

Hitting the Target

Born in 1786 in Eutin, Germany, Weber (*right*) was the son of an itinerant musician. From a tender age, he received music lessons, and had his first opera, *Das Waldmädchen*, later renamed *Silvana*, performed when he was 14 years old. From 1804, Weber directed the opera companies of Breslau, Prague and Dresden, and often made himself unpopular with his innovative reforms. In 1811, he composed the successful comic opera, *Abu Hassan*, and *Der Freischütz* made him internationally famous. Always delicate, Weber died prematurely at age 39, of tuberculosis. He had been working at Covent Garden and was buried in London. Wagner had the body of his great compatriot taken home to Dresden 18 years later.

BLACK MAGIC

Whoever made magic bullets had to invoke demonic powers, as in the scene from *Der Freischütz* (*left*), and might use a range of weird methods. The lead for the bullets had to come from churchyard crucifixes and be mixed with such unlikely ingredients as filings from a chain used to hang a thief, splinters from an oak tree struck by lightning or a piece of red silk that had been threaded through the eyes of a toad. The lead then had to be poured out of the eye-sockets of the skull of a woman who had just given birth!

IN CONTEXT: DER FREISCHÜTZ

THE FIRST ROMANTIC

The premiere of *Der Freischütz* is considered the birthdate of German Romantic Opera, and Weber (*below*) its father. Having fought off the French under Napoleon, the German people were impatient for their own opera, which Weber's epitomized. The story was rich with their own legend, and tapped their deepest feelings about forests and folklore, even as the music swept them away with its romanticism: simplicity married to a soaring imagination. Weber paved the way for Wagner, who, for once, was all admiration. "Never has a more German musician lived than you!" he declared.

A FLYING START

This was the first opera to open at the new Schauspielhaus in Berlin, on June 18, 1821. The audience was so enraptured that wreaths and flowers flew at the end. Weber wrote that, "everything went excellently and was sung with love." This was followed by triumph in Vienna and in Dresden. By 1824, three versions were competing for audiences in London, and the year after, *Der Freischütz* was in New York. Berlioz brought it to the Paris Opéra in 1841, to huge acclaim. There were even affectionate parodies in German and English (illustration *above*).

KEY NOTES

In 1853, a Polish count, who had seen a production of Der Freischütz at the Paris Opéra, sued the company on the grounds that so many cuts and alterations had been made that he had not seen the original work. His suit was dismissed.

Credits & Acknowledgments

PICTURE CREDITS

Cover /Title and Contents Pages/ IBC: Bridgeman Art Library, London/The Detroit Institute of Arts, USA. Founders Society purchase with Mr & Mrs Bert L. Smokler & Mr & Mrs Lawrence A. Fleischman funds (Henry Fuseli: The Nightmare, 1781)
AKG London: 13(r), 14(r), 19(c), 20(t), 22(r), 24(l)
Horst Maack 2 & 4(b); Bridgeman Art Library, London/Victoria & Albert Museum, London 12(r); Mary Evans Picture Library: 16(t); Lebrecht Collection: 3(c), 8(l), 11(c), 13(l), 17(t), 24(r), 25(t & b); M-Press Picture Library: 16(b); Performing Arts Library/Clive Barda 6(l & r), 9(c), 10, 12(l), 14(l), 15(r), 21(t & b), 22(l), 23(b); Photostage/Donald Cooper 18, 20(b); Reg Wilson: 4(t), 5(l & r), 7(l & r), 8(r), 15(l), 17(b), 23(t).

All illustrations and symbols: John See